S0-AIK-681

Centered on Learning

FALL

Over 90 Terrific Seasonal Center Ideas

Table of Contents

More learning center books from The Mailbox®

Project Editors: Michele M. Stoffel Menzel, Hope H. Taylor
Staff Editors: Cindy K. Daoust, Sherri Lynn Kuntz, Elizabeth H. Lindsay, Susan Walker
Copy Editors: Gina Farago, Karen Brewer Grossman, Karen L. Huffman, Amy Kirtley, Debbie Shoffner
Cover Artists: Kimberly Richard, Nick Greenwood
Art Coordinator: Rebecca Saunders
Artists: Pam Crane, Nolan Galloway, Theresa Lewis Goode, Sheila Krill, Mary Lester, Kimberly Richard, Rebecca Saunders
Typesetters: Lynette Maxwell, Mark Rainey

President, The Mailbox Book Company™: Joseph C. Bucci
Book Development Managers: Stephen Levy, Elizabeth H. Lindsay, Thad McLaurin, Susan Walker
Book Planning Manager: Chris Poindexter
Curriculum Director: Karen P. Shelton
Traffic Manager: Lisa K. Pitts
Librarian: Dorothy C. McKinney
Editorial and Freelance Management: Karen A. Brudnak
Editorial Training: Irving P. Crump
Editorial Assistants: Terrie Head, Melissa B. Montanez, Hope Rodgers, Jan E. Witcher

www.themailbox.com

Manufactured in the United States
10 9 8 7 6 5 4 3 2

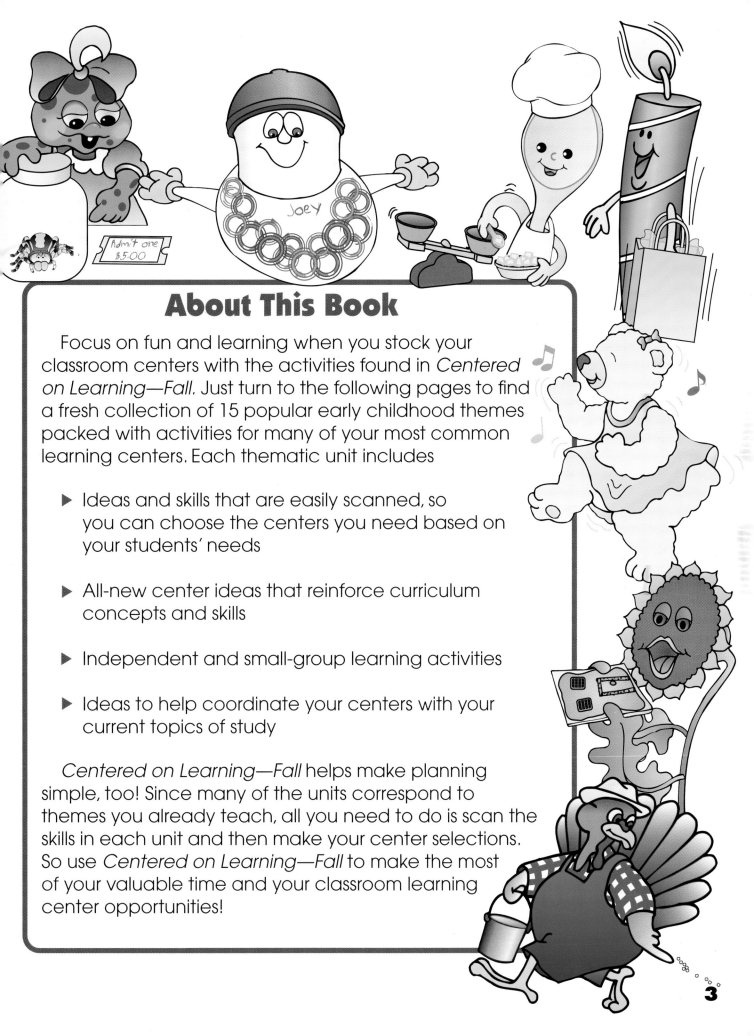

About This Book

Focus on fun and learning when you stock your classroom centers with the activities found in *Centered on Learning—Fall.* Just turn to the following pages to find a fresh collection of 15 popular early childhood themes packed with activities for many of your most common learning centers. Each thematic unit includes

▶ Ideas and skills that are easily scanned, so you can choose the centers you need based on your students' needs

▶ All-new center ideas that reinforce curriculum concepts and skills

▶ Independent and small-group learning activities

▶ Ideas to help coordinate your centers with your current topics of study

Centered on Learning—Fall helps make planning simple, too! Since many of the units correspond to themes you already teach, all you need to do is scan the skills in each unit and then make your center selections. So use *Centered on Learning—Fall* to make the most of your valuable time and your classroom learning center opportunities!

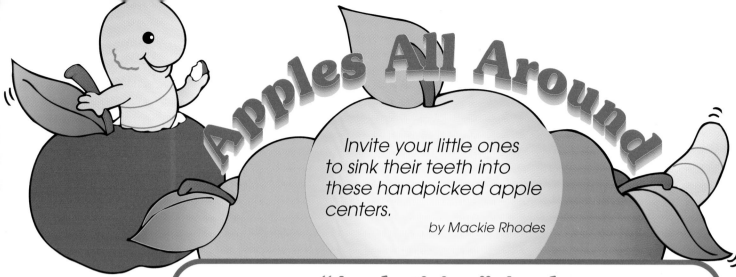

Apples All Around

Invite your little ones to sink their teeth into these handpicked apple centers.

by Mackie Rhodes

"Apple-tizing" Apples

Literacy Center

▶ *experience with text*
▶ *letter recognition*
▶ *left-to-right progression*

Your youngsters are sure to work up an appetite for apples as they polish their literacy skills at this juicy center! In advance, have students bring in different magazine pictures or drawings of different apple food items. Glue the pictures to a large apple cutout as shown; then label each picture. Place the cutout at a center along with a small basket of letter manipulatives. When a child visits the center, have him use the letters to form a word from the cutout. After "reading" the word, have him put the letters back in the basket and then continue in the same manner with the remaining words on the cutout.

Worm Workout

Sensory Center

▶ *tactile exploration*
▶ *fine motor*

It's time to give some worms a workout as your youngsters explore different textures! In advance, have a parent donate a bag of Gummy Worm® candies and several bags of dried apple chips. Put the worms in a plastic bowl and spread the apple chips on a baking sheet. Place the items at a center. Invite each child to make the worms crawl, hide, race, and tunnel through the apple chips. Whew! These worms are really moving!

4

Worms in My Apple!

Using this center idea is a great way to wiggle positional concepts into your curriculum! To prepare, paint a medium-sized Styrofoam® ball with a mixture of one part glue to two parts paint. When the paint is dry, use a pencil to poke two holes through the ball (apple); then use a permanent marker to outline each hole as shown. Fashion a stem and leaf using pipe cleaners and push them into the top of the apple. To make worms, bend long pipe cleaners in half; then twist them together. Place the items at a center. Invite each pair of students to take turns placing the worms *in, out, over, under, beside, around,* and *through* the apple as directed by his partner. Look at those worms go!

Math Center

understanding ◀
positional words
following directions ◀

Through!

Apple-Part Art

Here's a painting project that will result in an orchard of apple trees! Simply core several apples and then cut the cores in half as shown. Cut the remainders of the apples into thick slices. Place the apple parts at a center along with a class supply of white construction paper and shallow pans of brown, green, and red paint. To make an apple tree, a child first dips an apple slice into the brown paint and then presses it onto a piece of paper to form a trunk. Using a different apple slice and green paint, she repeats this process to paint the leaves. Next, she dips the flat end of the core into the red paint and then presses it among the leaves to create apples. When the paint is dry, display students' apple trees on a bulletin board. What a beautiful apple orchard!

Art Center

creative expression ◀
fine motor ◀

Apple Dough Twists

Apple dough is an "a-peel-ing" way to strengthen your little ones' fingers! In advance, follow the recipe below to make a batch of apple play dough; then place it at a center along with a baking sheet. Invite each child to roll two portions of dough between his fingers to make ropes. Next, have him press one end of each rope together and then twist them. Encourage him to place the apple twists on the baking sheet and pretend to bake them. They smell yummy!

Motor Skills Center

▶ *fine motor*
▶ *following directions*

Apple Dough

Ingredients:
2 c. flour
1 c. salt
1 c. apple juice
several drops of red, yellow, or green food coloring

Directions:
Mix the ingredients together in a large bowl. Add more flour or juice as needed until the desired consistency is achieved.

Apples With Character

Your youngsters will shine with pride as they create apple characters to use during pretend play! Simply place a variety of real or Styrofoam® apples at a center along with a selection of Mr. Potato Head® parts. Encourage each child to use the toy parts to create an apple character. Then invite him to use his prop to tell a story. As he does, he'll have the opportunity to strengthen his language skills. Now that's a happy ending!

Dramatic-Play Center

▶ *verbal expression*
▶ *creative expression*

Once upon a time there were two apples...

who lived with their granny.

Apple Bowls

These edible bowls can hold almost any snack! In advance, create a class supply of apple bowls by cutting apples in half and then scooping out the center of each apple half. Dip the bowls in lemon juice and place them at a center along with plastic utensils, snack items such as peanut butter or yogurt, and toppings such as sprinkles, cinnamon, and raisins. When a child visits the center, she fills her bowl with the desired snack item and then adds a topping. You're sure to hear lots of crunching and munching as your little ones eat their entire snacks—including the bowls!

Cooking Center

sensory exploration ◀
decision making ◀

Apple Bubble Blowers

Involve your students in discovering how an apple can be used to make beautiful bubble paintings. In advance, follow the recipe below to make a batch of colorful bubble mixture. Pour the mixture into a shallow pan and place it at a center along with a class supply of cored apples (see illustration) and a class supply of white construction paper. When a child visits this center, she grasps an apple with both hands and dips one end into the bubble mixture. Then she lifts the apple and blows through the other end so that the bubbles pop onto a sheet of paper, creating a colorful print. This apple center is sure to be popular!

Science Center

investigation ◀
creative expression ◀

Colorful Bubble Mixture
In each pan mix:
5 tbsp. soft water (or distilled)
4 tbsp. clear Dawn® dish detergent
5 or more drops of a different food coloring

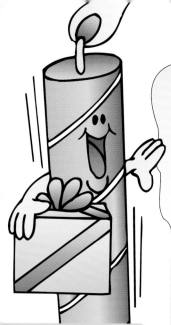

It's a Birthday Bash!

Wrap the presents, light the candles, and put on your party clothes. It's birthday party time and everyone is invited!

by Kim Love

Math Center

▶ matching numerals to corresponding sets
▶ counting

How Many Candles?

Here's an activity that adds up to counting skills worth celebrating! Simply stock a center with cupcake liners, play dough, a supply of index cards numbered from 1 to 15, and 15 birthday candles. When a child visits the center, he fills a liner with play dough to resemble a cupcake. Next, he selects a card and puts the matching number of candles on the cupcake. To continue play, he removes the candles and then repeats the activity using different number cards. Now that's counting fun!

Art Center

▶ fine motor
▶ following directions

Hats Off to Birthdays!

Celebrate little ones' creativity with these festive party hats! In advance, stock a center with lengths of curling ribbon, tape, a class supply of 9" x 12" sheets of construction paper, a shallow pan of thinned glue, large paint-brushes, confetti, a stapler, a hole puncher, and pipe cleaners. To make a hat, a child tapes several lengths of ribbon onto a sheet of construction paper as shown. Next, she paints a layer of glue on the opposite side and then sprinkles the paper with confetti. When the glue is dry, help her form a cone shape to resemble a hat; then staple it in place. Punch a hole in each of the two bottom corners. Insert a pipe cleaner through each hole; then twist to secure. Invite young-sters to put on their hats and loosely twist the pipe cleaners around their chins. That's quite a party hat!

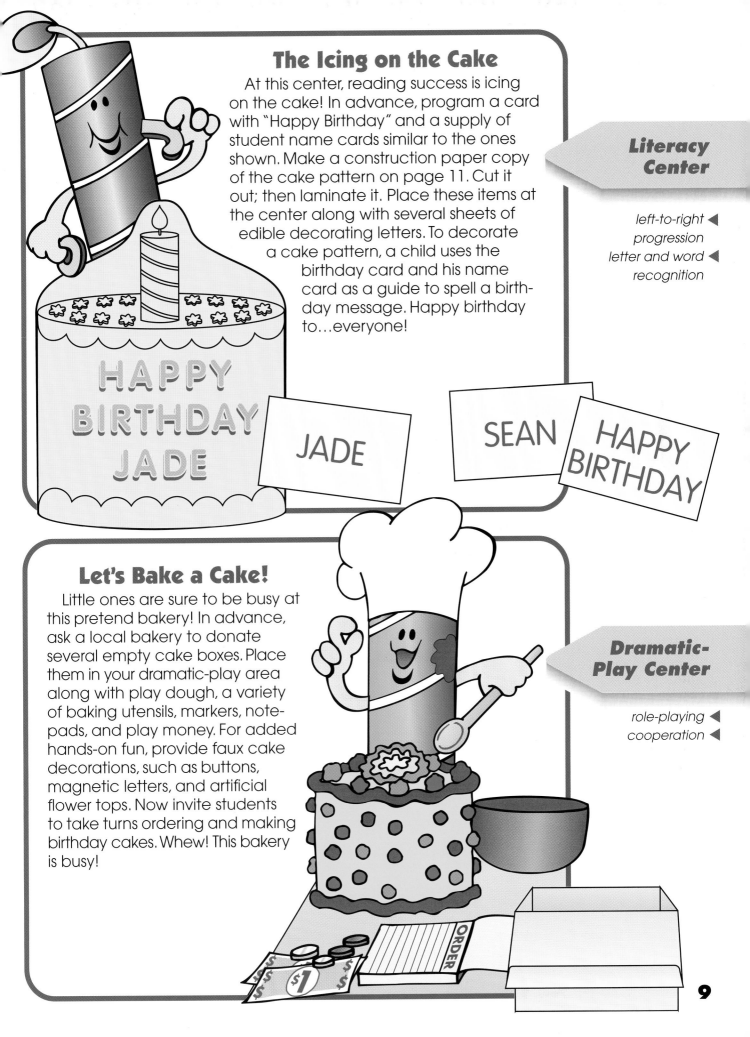

The Icing on the Cake

At this center, reading success is icing on the cake! In advance, program a card with "Happy Birthday" and a supply of student name cards similar to the ones shown. Make a construction paper copy of the cake pattern on page 11. Cut it out; then laminate it. Place these items at the center along with several sheets of edible decorating letters. To decorate a cake pattern, a child uses the birthday card and his name card as a guide to spell a birthday message. Happy birthday to...everyone!

Literacy Center

left-to-right ◄
progression
letter and word ◄
recognition

HAPPY BIRTHDAY JADE

JADE

SEAN

HAPPY BIRTHDAY

Let's Bake a Cake!

Little ones are sure to be busy at this pretend bakery! In advance, ask a local bakery to donate several empty cake boxes. Place them in your dramatic-play area along with play dough, a variety of baking utensils, markers, note-pads, and play money. For added hands-on fun, provide faux cake decorations, such as buttons, magnetic letters, and artificial flower tops. Now invite students to take turns ordering and making birthday cakes. Whew! This bakery is busy!

Dramatic-Play Center

role-playing ◄
cooperation ◄

ORDER

$1

A Lot of Air

Use this activity to involve your youngsters in experimenting with motion! To prepare, use masking tape to create a starting line and a finish line at a center tabletop. Stock the center with party items of various weights, such as a paper plate, a wrapped box, and a cupcake liner. When a child visits the center, have her place an object on the starting line and then try to blow it across the finish line. After she tests the objects, have her sort them into two piles based on whether they blew across the finish line or not. One, two, three—blow!

Discovery Center

▶ *motion exploration*
▶ *sorting*

START   FINISH

Sensory Center

▶ *tactile discrimination*
▶ *analytical thinking*

What's Inside the Birthday Bag?

Pique your youngsters' curiosity with these mystery birthday bags! In advance, fill your sensory table with tissue paper and colorful recycled gift bags. Place a different party item, such as a plastic spoon or a birthday candle, in each bag. Then cover each object with a piece of crumpled tissue paper. When a child visits the center, have her use her sense of touch to guess the contents of each bag. Next, have her peek inside the bag to check her guess. Surprise! It's a spoon!

Color Me Happy!

Brighten up your centers with the following colorful activities.

by Roxanne LaBell Dearman

Literacy Center

▶ color discrimination
▶ color word recognition

Digging Into Color

Your youngsters are sure to dig into this color word and sorting activity. Add sand to a plastic storage container along with shovels and small colorful items such as beads, blocks, and crayons. Then program index cards with color words or colored shapes. Invite youngsters to search for objects that match the words or shapes on their cards. Ready, set, dig in!

Art Center

▶ creative expression
▶ fine motor

Peaceful Painting

Encourage your budding artists with this creative activity. In advance, gather watercolor paints, brushes, and newsprint. Place these items in your art area along with a bowl containing plastic fruits. If desired, play some calm classical background music. Encourage youngsters to observe the fruit bowl and then paint what they see on their papers. Allow the paintings to dry; then display them for all to enjoy.

Soakin' Up the Colors

Watch your youngsters' amazement grow by leaps and bounds with this colorful experiment! First, share *White Rabbit's Color Book* by Alan Baker. Then use the pattern on page 15 to make a class supply of rabbit cutouts from coffee filters. In each of three bowls, combine water and several drops of red, yellow, or blue food coloring. Place the bowls, three eyedroppers, and newspaper at a center. When a child visits the center, she places her rabbit on a sheet of newspaper. Then she gently squeezes different-colored water drops on the rabbit and observes the change. Rainbow rabbits abound!

Discovery Center

investigation ◄
fine motor ◄

Flashes of Color

Illuminate youngsters' patterning skills with this flashy activity! Create a color mat by cutting out three circles from a shoebox lid, as shown. Tape a different color of cellophane over each resulting opening. Then program index cards with different color patterns using the colors on the mat. Display the mat, the index cards, and a flashlight at a center. Invite each child to copy or extend the pattern on each card by shining the flashlight through the corresponding colors. Challenge older students to create original color patterns.

Math Center

patterning ◄
color identification ◄

Colorful Hide-and-Seek

Ready or not, here comes a sensory center that's sure to have youngsters searching for colors. Partially fill several resealable plastic bags with a sensory material, such as shaving cream, rice, potting soil, or flour. Add a different-colored button to each bag; then seal. Use masking tape to reinforce the seal. Encourage youngsters to shake, squeeze, and roll the sensory bags until they discover each hidden button. Button, button, who found a blue button?

Sensory Center

► *fine motor*
► *sensory experience*
► *color identification*

Mystery Mix

Color mixing is a treat when youngsters whip up this pretty pudding! Stock a center with a class supply of plastic spoons, vanilla pudding cups, and the color-mixing cards on the bottom of page 15. Also provide red, yellow, and blue food coloring. To make a mystery pudding, a child selects a card, reads the color words, and colors the first two circles. (For younger children, color the cards beforehand.) Next, the child squeezes a few drops of food coloring into her pudding according to the recipe directions. Then she uses a spoon to mix the two colors together to create a new color. After stirring, she colors the remaining circle to match the color. What a colorful treat!

Cooking Center

► *following directions*
► *color identification*
► *color word recognition*

Rabbit Pattern
Use with "Soakin' Up the Colors" on page 13.

Color-Mixing Cards
Use with "Mystery Mix" on page 14.

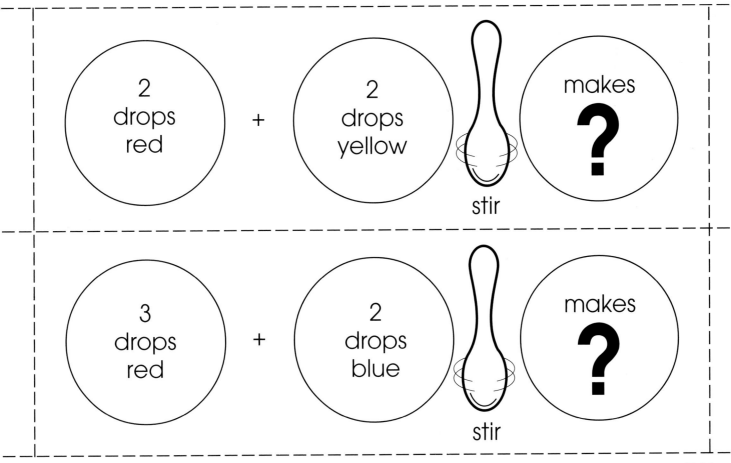

A Peek at Babies

Peekaboo! It's time for youngsters to have bundles of fun learning about babies with these creative center ideas.

by Valerie Corbeille

Look What Babies Can Do!

From crying to crawling, babies can do lots of things during their first year. Use this literacy center to help your youngsters better understand this. Stock your center with several picture books about babies, such as *Baby! Talk!* by Penny Gentieu. When a student pair visits the center, have the twosome look at a picture book together and describe what the babies are doing. Look! That baby is yawning!

Literacy Center

▶ experience with literature
▶ verbal expression

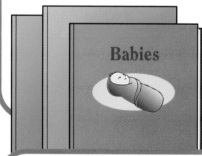

Twist and Turn

Put a new twist on strengthening fine-motor and thinking skills with this baby bottle activity! In advance, have parents donate a supply of clean baby bottles. Take the bottles apart and place the pieces at a center. Invite youngsters to put the bottles together and take them apart again. Twist and turn—it's a baby bottle!

Motor Center

▶ fine motor
▶ problem solving

Newborn Vision

This discovery idea is sure to give youngsters firsthand experience with how a newborn infant sees. To prepare, have parents donate several inexpensive children's sunglasses (with light-colored lenses) and a jar of petroleum jelly. Smear a thin layer of the jelly on the outside of the lenses of each pair of glasses; then place the glasses at a center along with a variety of black and white construction paper shapes. Ahead of time, explain to each small group that very young babies have blurry vision and have an easier time viewing high-contrast items. Then have students don glasses and look at the different shapes.

Discovery Center

investigation ◄
comparing ◄

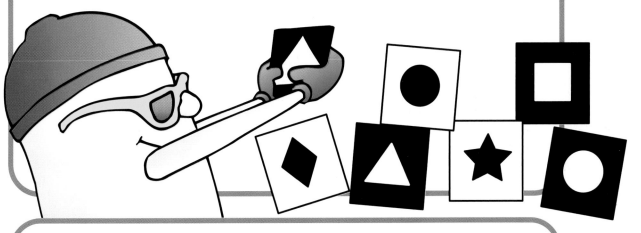

Baby Bottle Bibs

Capture your youngsters' creativity with this unique art project! To prepare, cut a class supply of paper plates to resemble bibs (see illustration). Then place the bibs at a center along with shallow containers of paint and clean baby bottle nipples. To decorate a bib, instruct a child to place a baby bottle nipple (flat side down) in the paint and then make prints on her bib. When the paint dries, encourage her to personalize her work. Ahhh, what precious little baby bibs!

Art Center

creative expression ◄
hand-eye ◄
coordination

Baby Socks

Little feet are sure to scamper to this math center that focuses on sorting baby socks! In advance, have parents donate pairs of different-colored infant socks. Place them in a basket along with a supply of spring-type clothespins. Then suspend a four-foot length of clothesline between two chairs as shown. When a child visits the center, have him match each pair of socks and then hang the pair on the clothesline. For added fun, have him pattern the socks by color. Oh, my! That's lots of socks!

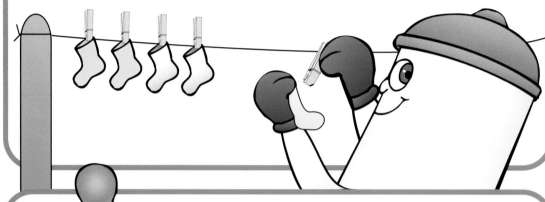

Rock-a-Bye Baby

Engage your youngsters in some imaginative play and you're sure to see lots of cuddling, patting, and whispering! Stock your dramatic-play area with dolls and actual baby supplies, such as a car seat, a diaper bag, infant clothes, baby blankets, and teething toys. Invite little ones to care for the infants. Hush, little baby. It's time to go nighty-night!

18

Splish, Splash—Baby Baths!

Your youngsters are sure to agree that babies need baths! Use this sensory activity to involve your little ones in the experience of bathing an infant. Half-fill your water table (or a large plastic tub) with water and then add a small

amount of bubble bath. Place plastic dolls, washcloths, and bath towels at the center. Then invite your little ones to wash and dry the babies. As they play, encourage them to name common body parts, such as ears, toes, and fingers. If desired, have parents donate some newborn pajamas so that your little ones can dress the babies after bath time. Splish, splash!

Sensory Center

sensory experience ◄
fine motor ◄

Baby Food Taste Test

Yummy or yucky? Your youngsters will be able to answer this question after they prepare and taste some homemade baby food! In advance, program a sheet of paper with the recipe as shown. Pour the box of baby rice cereal into a large plastic bowl. Half-fill a plastic pitcher with lukewarm water and place it at a center along with the bowl, the empty cereal box, two 1/4-cup measuring cups, a class supply of disposable bowls and spoons, and a class supply of Rice Krispies Treats®. When a child visits the center, have her follow the recipe to make a portion of rice cereal in a small bowl. After she tastes it, invite the student to taste a Rice Krispies Treat. Which tastes better? No doubt, your little ones will be glad that they no longer eat just baby food!

Cooking Center

following directions ◄
measuring ◄
exploration ◄

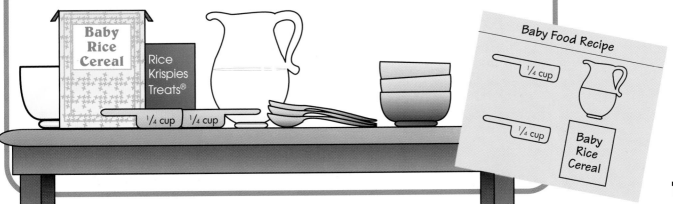

19

Lots of Leaves!

Jump right into a pile of autumn-related activities with these "unbe-leaf-able" centers!

by Audrey McNeill

Jump In!

Get little ones involved in patterning practice using layers of lovely fall leaves! Simply half-fill a wading pool (or sensory table) with a variety of real leaves. As each child visits the center, have her sort the leaves by shape, color, or size. Then have her use the sorted cards to make patterns. What fantastic fall foliage fun!

Sensory Center

▶ discrimination
▶ sorting
▶ patterning

Piles and Piles of Leaves

Rake up some fall fun for your youngsters with this literacy idea! In advance, make 20 construction paper copies of the leaf patterns on page 23; then cut them out. Program each of five paper lunch bags with a different consonant. Next, cut out magazine pictures of items that begin with the letter on each bag. If desired, include some extra pictures that do not match any of the bags. Glue each picture on a leaf cutout. Place these items at a center along with a toy rake. When a child visits the center, have him scatter the leaves and then rake them into a pile. Next, have him sort the leaves by putting them into their matching bags. For younger children, simply scatter leaves with labeled pictures; then encourage your students to "read" each picture. Now that's "unbe-leaf-able" prereading practice!

Literacy Center

▶ phonemic awareness
▶ letter-sound association
▶ vocabulary development

Five Fluttering Leaves

Flitter, flutter! Youngsters are sure to be whisked away by this listening center activity! In advance, make a recording of the poem below. Place the recording and five real or paper leaves at a center. Then recite the poem with your students. Invite each child to visit the center and act out the poem as she listens to the recording. If desired, print the poem on sentence strips and have students sequence them as they listen to the poem. Watch out for falling leaves!

Listening Center

listening ◄
following ◄
directions

Five Fluttering Leaves

Five fall leaves,
Green is what they wore.
One fluttered to the ground.
Now there are four.

Four fall leaves
Are as big as they can be.
The rain washes one away.
Now there are three.

Three fall leaves,
Turning colors in the dew.
The wind blows one away.
Now there are two.

Two fall leaves,
Hanging in the sun.
One lets go.
Now there is one.

One last leaf—
Now its time is done.
It flips and flutters to the ground.
Now there are none.

Splattered With Fall Colors

This art activity will add an array of autumn colors to your classroom! In advance, gather a class supply of real leaves. Use rolled tape to secure each leaf to the center of a 9" x 12" sheet of white construction paper. Place the papers at a center along with a shallow box and several spray bottles of thinned red, yellow, and orange paint. When a child visits the center, have her place a paper in the box (leaf side up) and then use the bottles to spray-paint her paper. When the paint is dry, carefully remove the leaf. Display both the splattered leaves and the colorful outlines to make a fantastic fall bulletin board. Look at those autumn hues!

Art Center

fine motor ◄
creative expression ◄

- *one-to-one correspondence*
- *counting*

Falling for Leaves

Little ones will gather up counting skills with this leafy activity! Place a die, a supply of small paper leaves, and one copy of the tree pattern on page 23 at a center. Have each child who visits the center place all of the leaves on the tree. Next, have him roll the die, count the dots, and remove the corresponding number of leaves from the tree. When the tree is bare, the activity is complete. Ooooh! Cooler weather is coming!

- *observation*
- *creativity*

Fabulous Fall Leaves

Orange, yellow, red, and brown—autumn leaves are all around! To prepare for this science center, duplicate a class supply of construction paper leaves using the leaf patterns on page 23. Place the leaves at the center along with a variety of real leaves. Also provide magnifying glasses, a class supply of six-inch plastic-wrap squares, and squeezable bottles of red and yellow paint. When a child visits the center, have her use a magnifying glass to observe the veins in the real autumn leaves. Then have her squirt a small amount of each color of paint onto a paper leaf. Next, have her place a piece of plastic wrap over her painted leaf and crinkle the wrap. When the paint is dry, have the child remove the plastic wrap to reveal a colorful leaf with realistic-looking veins!

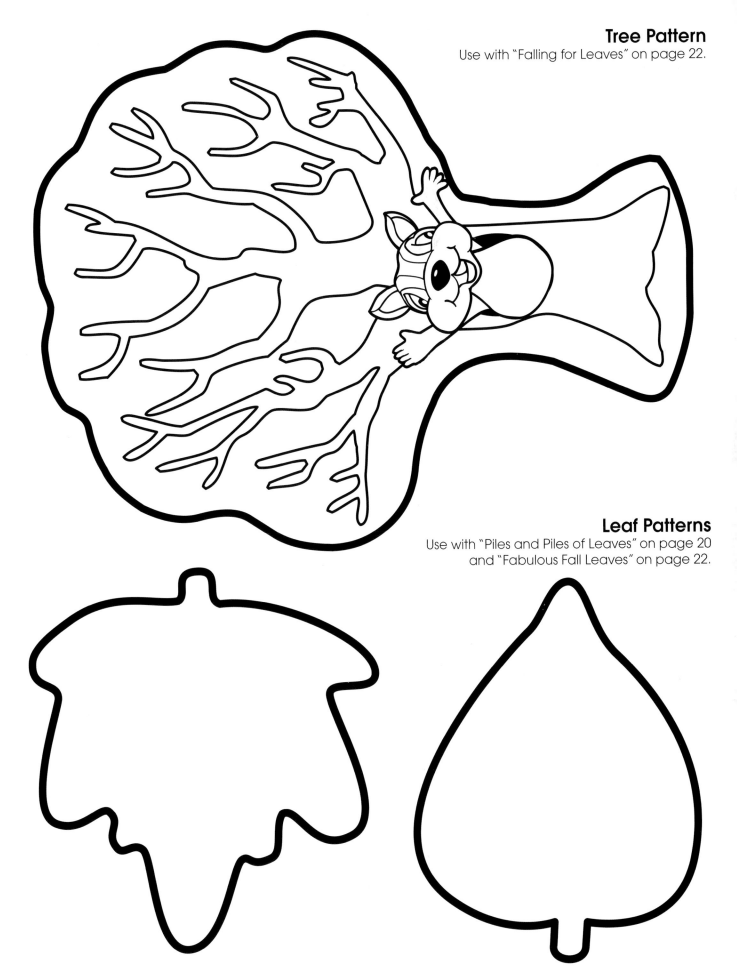

Tree Pattern
Use with "Falling for Leaves" on page 22.

Leaf Patterns
Use with "Piles and Piles of Leaves" on page 20
and "Fabulous Fall Leaves" on page 22.

Nothing but Nuts!

Crack open the wonders of nuts with your youngsters at these nifty centers!

by Sherri Lynn Kuntz

Literacy Center

▶ name recognition
▶ left-to-right progression

Nutty Names

"Nuttin'" but fun will be had by all when you reinforce name recognition skills with this activity! To prepare, use glue to print each student's name on a separate sheet of construction paper; then sprinkle the papers with chopped nuts. When the glue is dry, shake off the excess nuts and display the papers on a wall at youngsters' eye level. Then encourage your students to find and finger-trace their classmates' names as well as their own!

Math Center

▶ matching numerals to corresponding sets
▶ counting

Toss It to the Squirrels!

Nourish your youngsters' math skills with this gathering and sorting activity. In advance, scatter nuts throughout your math center. Make several construction paper copies of the squirrel and paw patterns on page 27 (enlarge if desired). Color the patterns and cut them out. Then glue each squirrel and a set of paws onto a tissue box as shown. Label each box with a different number and then place the box in your math center along with a large bowl. Invite each pair of students to use the bowl to collect the nuts and then feed the squirrels by tossing the corresponding number of nuts into each box. Chitter, chatter!

Wondering About Walnuts?

The walnut is the center of this observation activity! Place some unshelled walnuts, walnut halves, walnut meat, and walnut flavored cookies at a center. Invite youngsters to use their five senses to investigate the walnuts (beware of nut allergies). Then encourage each child to describe what she observed about the nuts!

Science Center

observation ◄
verbal expression ◄

Dramatic-Play Center

role-playing ◄
following directions ◄

Nuts, Anyone?

Students are sure to scamper to this nutty dramatic-play center! To create a nut store, stock a center with paper lunch bags, scoops or wooden spoons, notebooks, pencils, and a scale. Also provide several labeled bowls of nuts. Invite students to take turns pretending to be the customer and the storekeeper as they practice placing and filling orders. One scoop or two?

Let's Hear It for the Nut Band!

Delight your music enthusiasts with these rhythmic nut shakers! Make several different-colored nut shakers by pouring one spoonful of chopped nuts and a pinch of powdered tempera paint into each of several clear film canisters. Secure the lids; then shake the canisters. Make a recording of the song below and put it at the listening center. Invite each child to sing along with the recording and act out the song. Encourage him to sing the song several times, each time substituting a different color in place of the underlined word below. For older children, supply color word cards to help them determine the next color in the song. Shake, shake, shake it up!

(sung to the tune of "The Muffin Man")

Listen to the (green) nut band,
The (green) nut band, the (green) nut band.
Listen to the (green) nut band
And this is what you'll hear! *(shake, shake, shake)*

Music Center

▶ color discrimination
▶ sound discrimination

Nutty About Nuts

Set up this center and your little ones are sure to dig right in! Fill the sensory table (or a large plastic tub) with leaves, twigs, nutshells, and a variety of unshelled nuts for a realistic outdoor experience. Provide tongs and a large plastic bowl. Encourage your students to bury the nuts and then use the tongs to dig for them. After your youngsters have placed all the nuts in the bowl, have them bury the nuts again. Now that's fun in a nutshell!

Sensory Center

▶ fine motor
▶ tactile exploration

27

Fire Safety First!

Your youngsters are sure to learn important emergency skills as they enjoy a swift ride through these fire safety centers.

by Valerie R. Corbeille

Hot Hide-and-Seek

Literacy Center

▶ word recognition
▶ experience with text

Your little ones will develop a flair for word recognition with this prereading activity. To prepare, print "fire" on several index cards using uppercase and lowercase letters and different text styles. Place the cards at the center along with your favorite fire safety books. Invite each child to choose one card and one book. Then encourage her to use the card to help her find the word *fire* throughout the book. If desired, ask her to count the number of times she finds the word.

fire   FIRE   **fire**

Fire Hose Lineup

Math Center

▶ size discrimination
▶ sequencing

Size up your youngsters' discrimination skills with this math center. Cut drinking straws into five different lengths (one, two, three, four, and five inches) so that there is one of each length for each child. Then sort the straws by size into five separate containers. Place the containers, clear tape, and a class supply of 6" x 9" sheets of construction paper at a center. Direct each child to arrange the straws (fire hoses) in order from largest to smallest on a sheet of paper and then secure each one with tape. Now that's quite a lineup!

Firefighters' Footwear

Why do firefighters wear rubber boots? Have your little ones put this question to the test with this water experiment. In advance, gather a plastic tub, a water-filled spray bottle, and several different kinds of material squares (such as nylon, wool, rubber, canvas, and fleece). Encourage a child to predict which fabrics will *absorb* the water and which fabrics will *repel* the water. Have the child test her predictions by placing each piece of fabric into the tub. Then invite her to spray water onto the fabric pieces and observe the results. So that's why firefighters wear rubber boots!

Science Center

observation skills ◄
predicting ◄
outcomes

Shapely Fire Engines

Shape up youngsters' correspondence skills with these fun fire engines. To prepare, make several tagboard templates in different shapes. Place the shapes along with construction paper, scissors, glue, and crayons at a center. Post a picture of a fire engine for youngsters to observe. Then invite a child to create his own fire engine. (For younger students, precut the construction paper shapes.) Have him arrange the shapes and then glue them onto a sheet of construction paper. My, that's a shapely fire engine!

Art Center

shape recognition ◄
creativity ◄

▶ *role-playing*
▶ *gross motor*

Flames Out!

Turn your dramatic-play center into a practice zone for this fire safety technique. Place a mat or carpet on the floor near this center and add a sturdy sign with the word FIRE. Then encourage pairs of students to visit the center. Ask one student to hold up the sign while the other practices putting out the flames by acting out "Stop, Drop, and Roll." What a valuable lifesaving lesson!

Fire Hose Fill-Up

Your little firefighters are sure to enjoy pouring and exploring water with imaginary fire hoses. Display plastic funnels, plastic pitchers, and several different lengths of clear plastic tubing at a water table. If desired, add glitter to the water to emphasize visual discrimination. Next, invite a child to attach a funnel to a piece of tubing and then pour water into the funnel. For added fun, have him tie a knot in the middle of a piece of tubing. Again, invite him to pour water into the tube. Have him watch what happens after each pouring.

▶ *sensory experience*
▶ *investigation*

Dalmatian Pup Cups

What's white with black spots? This delicious yogurt treat that has students practicing measurement skills! To prepare, gather a large carton of vanilla yogurt, a package of mini chocolate chips, a half-cup measure, a tablespoon, and a class supply of clear plastic cups and spoons. Place these items at a center along with colorful permanent markers. Instruct each child to use a marker to draw a dalmatian puppy face onto his plastic cup as shown. To make a treat, a child simply measures a half-cup of yogurt into his cup and then stirs in two tablespoons of chocolate chips. Yum! It's chow time!

Cooking Center

following directions ◀
measuring ◀

Fire Station Setup

Build cooperation skills as youngsters construct their very own fire station. Stock a block center with toys, such as fire trucks, people, ladders, bells, and a dalmatian dog. Invite a small group of youngsters to work together to build a fire station that has windows, doors, and a garage. As they play, encourage the group to use related vocabulary, such as *siren, alarm, fire extinguisher,* and *exit.* Brring! Brring! Sound the alarm!

Block Center

fine motor ◀
verbal skills ◀
cognitive skills ◀
cooperation ◀

Spiders in the Spotlight

Incorporate some eight-legged fun into your classroom activities with these hands-on ideas!

by Sherri Lynn Kuntz

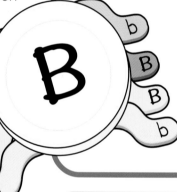

Spider Soup

You're sure to serve a huge helping of alphabet fun with this spider matching activity. In advance, use a permanent marker to print a different letter on each of several small plastic lids (spider bodies). Duplicate the spider leg patterns on page 35 to make four construction paper sets for each body. Program each set with matching letters (as shown) or words and then laminate the legs for durability. Place the spider parts in a large pot; then place it at the center along with a pair of tongs and a wide-bottomed plastic bowl. Have each child use the tongs to put a spider body into the bowl. Next, have her use the tongs to find the spider's matching legs and place them underneath its body. It won't be long before the soup pot's empty!

How Many Spider Eggs?

Count on generating enthusiasm for learning with this spider egg activity. In advance, make at least ten copies of the spider egg sac pattern on page 35. Write a different number on each spider and then place the spiders at a center along with mini marshmallows (spider eggs). Instruct students to put the appropriate number of eggs in each spider's sac. For a job well done, invite your little ones to sample some pretend spider eggs. Wow! That spider has four spider eggs!

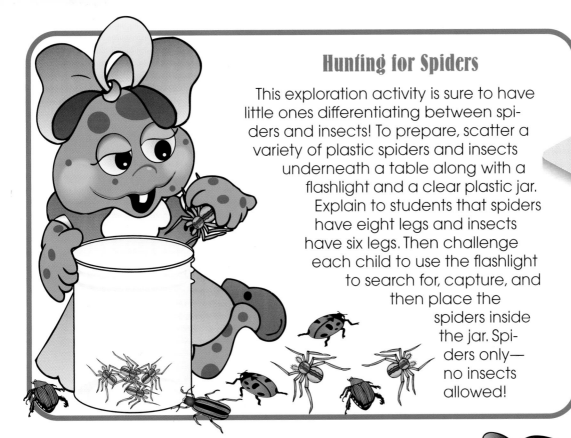

Hunting for Spiders

This exploration activity is sure to have little ones differentiating between spiders and insects! To prepare, scatter a variety of plastic spiders and insects underneath a table along with a flashlight and a clear plastic jar. Explain to students that spiders have eight legs and insects have six legs. Then challenge each child to use the flashlight to search for, capture, and then place the spiders inside the jar. Spiders only— no insects allowed!

Discovery Center

visual discrimination ◄
sorting ◄

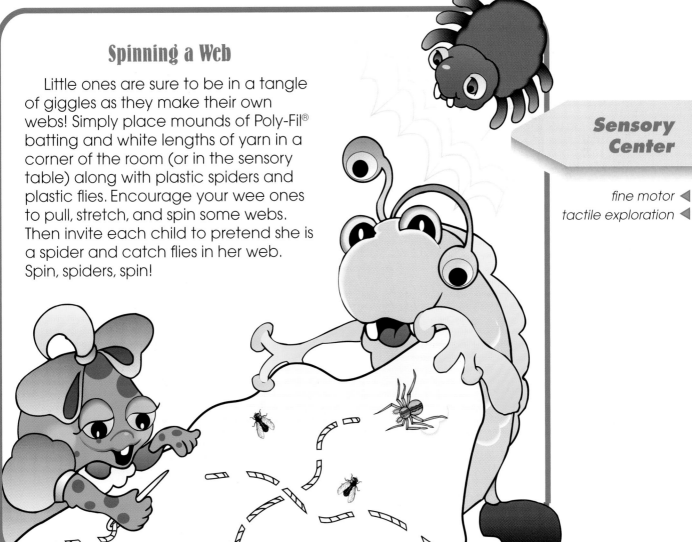

Spinning a Web

Little ones are sure to be in a tangle of giggles as they make their own webs! Simply place mounds of Poly-Fil® batting and white lengths of yarn in a corner of the room (or in the sensory table) along with plastic spiders and plastic flies. Encourage your wee ones to pull, stretch, and spin some webs. Then invite each child to pretend she is a spider and catch flies in her web. Spin, spiders, spin!

Sensory Center

fine motor ◄
tactile exploration ◄

Spider Museum

Establish a classroom museum filled with all kinds of spiders! In advance, have students draw and color large spiders on a piece of poster board. Display the poster in a designated area. Provide a variety of plastic spiders, Ping-Pong® balls (egg sacs), different-sized clear plastic jars, art supplies, spider books, and a pretend cash register. Encourage students to use the jars to make spider and egg sac displays. Then have them create labels, museum signs, tour guide badges, and admission tickets. Let the tours begin!

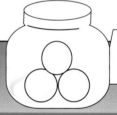

Where's the Spider?

Use this version of a familiar spider tune, and your little ones are sure to be caught up in music and movement! To prepare, display student photographs in the listening area. Then make a recording of the song below, each time using a different child's name. Place the recording at the listening center. Then invite each student to act out the song, using a pretend spider and his classmates' pictures. Sing for the spider—I spy one on your head!

(sung to the tune of "The Itsy-Bitsy Spider")

The itsy-bitsy spider went up on (child's name)'s head.
He turned all around and spun a nice soft web.
He crawled down (child's name)'s arm and jumped onto the floor.
Then the itsy-bitsy spider crawled to (child's name)'s head for more!

Spider Leg Patterns
Use with "Spider Soup" on page 32.

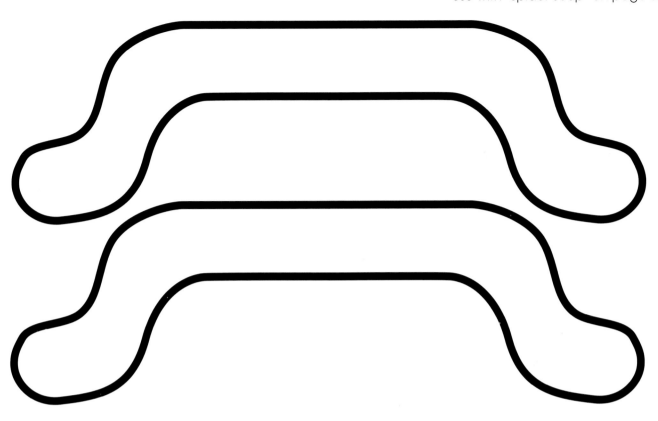

Spider Egg Sac Pattern
Use with "How Many Spider Eggs?" on page 32.

It's Pumpkin Patch Time!

Enrich your youngsters' harvest spirit with this plentiful patch of pumpkin ideas!

by Sandra Faulkner

Ooey-Gooey Pumpkin Pal

What's the scoop on pumpkin fun? This simple fine-motor activity! To make a pumpkin pal, use a permanent marker to draw a pumpkin outline on a large resealable bag. Next, squirt a dollop of shaving cream and a small amount of orange tempera paint into the bag. Seal the bag and use clear packaging tape to reinforce the seal. Invite a child to squish and squeeze the bag until an orange color appears. Next, have her use her finger to trace the pumpkin outline. Then encourage her to draw silly faces. Now "orange" you glad it's pumpkin time?

Motor Center

▶ tactile exploration
▶ fine motor

Jack-o'-Letters

Youngsters feel like blue-ribbon winners when they use these plump pumpkins to match letters! In advance, make nine construction paper copies of the pumpkin and triangle patterns on page 39. Cut them out; then laminate them. Use a permanent marker to print a different letter on each pumpkin eye and nose (leave the last nose blank). Then print a corresponding letter on each triangle piece. On the 27th triangle, print *Happy Halloween* (or *Happy Harvest*). Place the triangles inside a plastic pumpkin pail. Then invite a child to match the letters until each pumpkin face is complete. Happy, happy harvest!

Literacy Center

▶ letter matching
▶ following directions

36

How Does Your Pumpkin Grow?

Cultivate an interest in pumpkins with this discovery activity. In advance, have parents donate ripened and unripened pumpkins. Place the pumpkins at the center along with green curling ribbon and artificial greenery to represent vines. When your little ones visit the pumpkin patch, encourage them to observe the pumpkins. Then have them sort the pumpkins by size and color. What's on the vine? Why, it's the great green pumpkin!

Science Center

visual discrimination ◄
sorting ◄

"Kool" Pumpkin Pies

Spice up the sensory center with the delicious scent of fresh pumpkin pie! Follow the recipe below to make a batch of scented play dough. Place the dough and mini aluminum pie pans at the sensory table. When a child visits the center, have her create pretend pumpkin pies. No tasting please!

Sensory Center

sensory experience ◄
fine motor ◄

No-Cook Kool-Aid® Play Dough

Ingredients:
2 1/2 c. flour
1/2 c. salt
3 tbsp. cooking oil
1 tbsp. alum
3 tsp. ground cloves

1 c. boiling water
1 pkg. unsweetened Kool-Aid® (orange)
3 tsp. pumpkin pie spice

Directions:
Mix the ingredients in a large bowl. Add more flour or water until the desired consistency is achieved.

Counting Candy Teeth

Math
Center

▶ number recognition
▶ one-to-one correspondence

Your youngsters will be all aglow when you treat them to this sweet math center! In advance, make ten construction paper copies of the pumpkin and hat patterns on page 39. Print a different numeral on each hat. Next, draw a different number of teeth on each pumpkin to correspond with the numeral on each hat. Cut out the hats and the pumpkins; then laminate them. Place them at your center along with a bag of candy corn. (Make sure to have extras for sampling.) When a child visits the center, he matches a hat to the corresponding pumpkin and then places a piece of candy on each tooth. For younger children, glue each hat to its matching pumpkin and then have them practice number association by placing the corresponding number of candy pieces on each pumpkin's teeth. What sweet success!

"Boo-tiful" Paper Cup Pumpkins

Art
Center

▶ fine motor
▶ creative expression

Get youngsters grinning from ear to ear when they decorate these unique pumpkins! To prepare, punch a small hole through the center of the bottom of one plastic cup for each child. To create a pumpkin, a child paints the outside of her cup with thinned glue; then she covers the glue with orange and yellow tissue paper squares. Next, she glues wiggle eyes and beads to the inverted cup to make a pumpkin face. When the glue dries, she inserts a green pipe cleaner into the punched-out hole (tape to secure if necessary) and then twists it to resemble a pumpkin vine. That's a festive pumpkin!

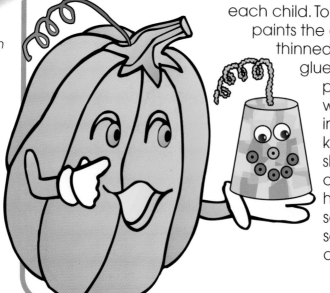

Pumpkin Pattern

Use with "Jack-o'-Letters" on page 36 and "Counting Candy Teeth" on page 38.

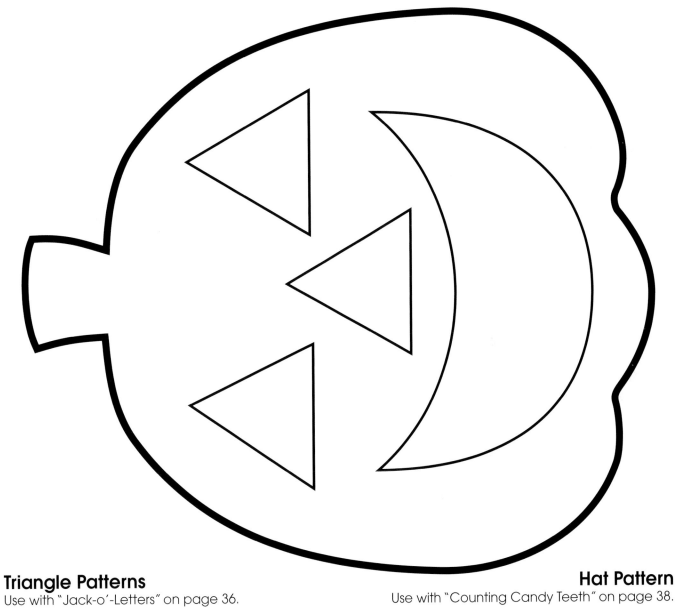

Triangle Patterns
Use with "Jack-o'-Letters" on page 36.

Hat Pattern
Use with "Counting Candy Teeth" on page 38.

Dinosaur Days!

These cross-curricular center ideas are sure to have your little ones thundering around with enthusiasm for those reptiles from long, long ago!

by Julie A. Koczur

Discovery Center

▶ investigation
▶ measurement
▶ problem solving

Dino Feet Can't Be Beat!

This activity is sure to have an enormous impact on how your little learners view the size of dinosaur feet! To prepare, use bulletin board paper to make a large footprint similar to the one shown. Next, invite youngsters to take off their shoes. Encourage them to arrange the shoes in a variety of ways to discover just how many shoes fit on the large dinosaur footprint. Stomp, stomp!

Art Center

▶ fine motor
▶ following directions

Prehistoric Puppets

These baby dinosaur puppets are sure to fill your room with bouncing bundles of prehistoric fun! Make a class supply of page 43 on green construction paper. Then fold one nine-inch paper plate in half for each child. Place these items at a center along with scissors, glue sticks, markers, wiggle eyes, and a completed sample. Direct each child to color a plate and then cut out the pattern pieces. Have him glue wiggle eyes to the head and then glue the pieces on his plate as shown. Then help him punch two holes in the rounded part of the plate as shown. Tie one end of each of two lengths of yarn through each hole and then tie the opposite ends around a craft stick. These dinosaurs are ready to dance!

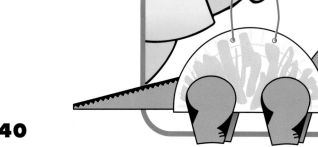

The Great Dinosaur Exploration!

Give your junior scientists a feel for what it was like to live in the time of the dinosaurs! To prepare the center, cover a small table with a blanket (cave), place a blue paper oval on the floor (pond), and stack several pillows (mountain or volcano). Put plastic dinosaurs, backpacks, maps, toy binoculars, and different-sized plastic eggs at the center. Encourage students to use their baby dinosaurs from "Prehistoric Puppets" on page 40 as they explore their surroundings. In no time, you're sure to have dinosaurs crawling, climbing, and stomping through the swamp. Roarrr!

Dramatic-Play Center

role playing ◀
creative thinking ◀

Story Swamp

Rev up your students' interest in this swampy atmosphere filled with dinosaur tales! Fill an inflated swimming pool with shredded newspaper. Then hide dinosaur books beneath the swampy grasses. It won't take long before your ferociously friendly dinosaur lovers climb in and read!

Literacy Center

experience with ◀
literature

Those Amazing Bones!

Your little archaeologists are sure to dig right into this "dino-mite" sand table! Bury items such as plastic bones, small rocks, shells, bark, and pebbles. For added fun, place a scale, magnifying glasses, rulers, clean paintbrushes (for dusting off finds), sieves, small plastic shovels, clipboards, paper, and pencils near the table. Then invite your young explorers to search for prehistoric items. No bones about it, digging is fun!

Sensory Center

▶ sensory experience
▶ exploration and discovery

In Shape With Dinosaurs

Youngsters' imaginations will run wild when they create these shapely dinosaurs! In advance, make dinosaur mats similar to the ones shown by tracing different tagboard shapes onto sheets of construction paper. Place the mats at a center along with construction paper shapes (cut to match the mats). A child selects a mat and then matches the manipulatives to the corresponding shapes on her mat. For added fun, encourage youngsters to use the manipulatives to make their own prehistoric creatures!

Math Center

▶ matching shapes

Stegosaurus

Diplodocus

Triceratops

Tyrannosaurus

legs

tail

head

A Place to Call Home

Gather your little ones and settle into some centers that are sure to build lots of learning fun!

by Melissa Hauck

Art
Center

▶ *creativity*
▶ *fine motor*

House Painting With a Twist

Here's a fresh idea that will help your youngsters brush up on their painting skills. Add a bit of lemon-flavored gelatin powder to your favorite paint colors. Also stock your art area with a few painter's caps, paint smocks, and a variety of paintbrushes and sponge brushes. Then invite each youngster to paint a house. As she does, she'll have the opportunity to practice painting shapes that form houses. Mmm. That's one lemony-fresh-smelling house!

Sensory
Center

▶ *tactile exploration*
▶ *fine motor*

Home, "Tweet" Home

Youngsters get a beakful of finger-strengthening exercise when they build these homes for birds! In advance, create bird beaks by gluing a yellow triangle of craft foam and two wiggle eyes to each of several clothespins. Then fill the sensory table with nest parts, such as twigs, feathers, leaves, string, and grass clippings. Encourage each youngster to use a beak to pick up and arrange the parts to form a nest. Here, birdie, birdie!

Shelter From the Storm

What roof would you want over your head in a rainstorm? Invite youngsters to decide after testing different roofing possibilities. Gather a variety of materials, such as fabrics, paper, cardboard, plastic, and wood. Cut the items into four- to six-inch squares. To make a house, remove the top from a pint-sized carton. Set the carton inside a cake pan. Then place the items in a center with a small watering can filled with water. When a child visits the center, he places a square (roof) on top of the carton and then sprinkles water (rain) over it. Next, he removes the roof to see if any water got inside the house. He continues testing several roofing materials. You may just have future roofers on your hands after several students discover the best ways to repel rain.

Discovery Center

investigation ◀
observation ◀

In the Neighborhood

Transform your math area into a neighborhood! To prepare, staple a four-inch-wide length of black or gray paper to a bulletin board to represent a street. Next, cut simple house shapes from colorful construction paper. Then write a different numeral from 1 to 5 (up to 10 for older children) on each house. Invite a small group to arrange the houses in numerical order above the road. Have them name the color of the *first* house. Then ask them to identify the colors of the *second* and *third* houses. Continue in this manner until the colors and positions of every house have been named. For added fun, invite a youngster to drive a toy car to a specific address.

Math Center

counting ◀
identifying ordinal ◀
numbers

A House for Me!

Here's a tasty treat that will give youngsters a chance to practice following directions! To prepare, make a copy of the recipe cards on page 47; then cut them out. Display the cards on a chart in your cooking area. Then gather the ingredients and supplies listed below and put them in your cooking area. Encourage youngsters to follow the directions to prepare the recipe. Who knew a house could be so tasty?

Cooking Center

▶ fine motor
▶ following directions

A House for Me!

Ingredients for each child:
1 graham cracker square
1 large spoonful of peanut butter
2 cereal squares
2 1/2 pretzel sticks
1 M&M's® chocolate candy

Supplies for each child:
1 plastic knife
napkin

Whose House?

After a shared reading of *A House Is a House for Me* by Mary Ann Hoberman, invite students to create their own version of this classic tale! Stock a center with crayons, white construction paper, and copies of the book. Then invite a child to write or dictate, "A (type of house) is a house for a (the house's occupant)," filling in the blanks as shown. Next, have her illustrate the sentence. Bind the completed pages into a book titled "Whose House?" Youngsters are sure to enjoy taking turns reading the new book!

Literacy Center

▶ vocabulary development
▶ retelling

Whose House?
Written & Illustrated by
Miss Hauck's Class

A _nest_ is a house for a _bird_.

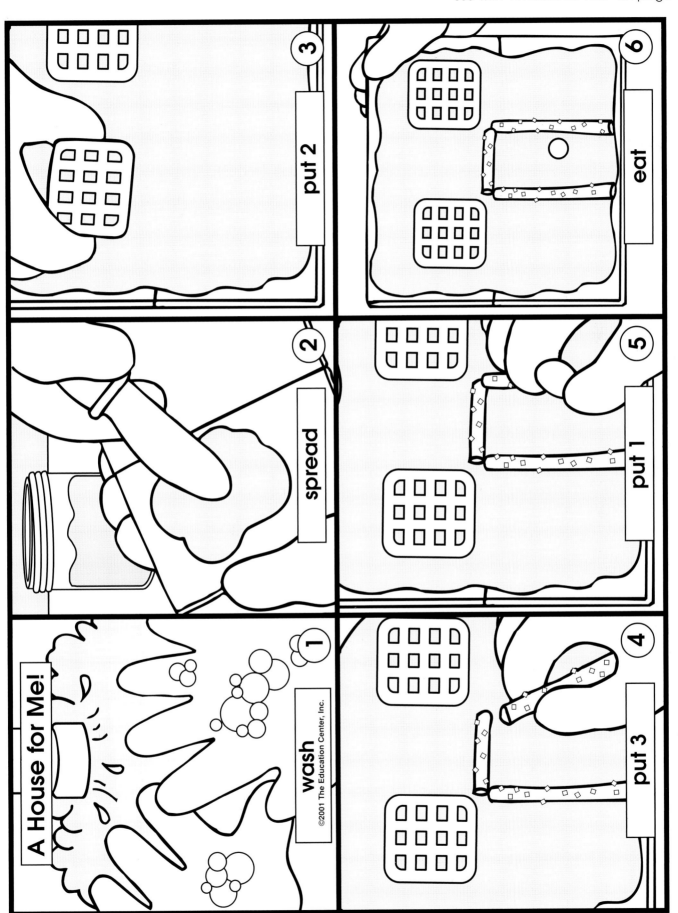

A House for Me!

wash
©2001 The Education Center, Inc.
1

spread
2

put 2
3

put 3
4

put 1
5

eat
6

Terrific Turkeys

Gobble, gobble! Your little ones are sure to learn more about turkeys as they visit the following terrific centers.

adapted from ideas by Kim Richman

Math Center

▶ *patterning*
▶ *size discrimination*

Nesting Numbers

Have your youngsters create "egg-citing" patterns with this clutch of eggs. To prepare, collect a Hula-Hoop® toy and a supply of small and large plastic eggs. Tell your little ones that turkey eggs are twice as big as chicken eggs. Then invite a small group to arrange the eggs in a pattern around the inside of the hoop. As they do, encourage them to describe the attributes they are using for patterning. You're sure to hear cheerful chants of "small egg, large egg, small egg, large egg!"

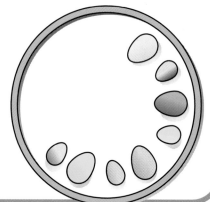

Science Center

▶ *fine motor*
▶ *exploration*

Scratch the Surface

Exploration is just a scratch away with this simulation of an instinctive turkey trait. To prepare, add sand to a plastic tub along with a cup of dried corn and several sand scrapers. Explain to your little ones that a turkey uses its claws to scratch the ground in search of food (corn, nuts, seeds, and roots). Invite a child to use a scraper to scratch through the sand in search of the hidden kernels of corn. Dig in!

Turkey Treats

In celebration of the turkey, use its favorite food to help your youngsters with measurement exploration. Fill your sensory table with dried corn and a variety of plastic cups, funnels, and containers. Then invite your youngsters to measure and pour the corn into different containers. Wow! That's a whole lot of turkey treats!

Sensory Center

tactile experience ◄
measuring ◄
fine motor ◄

Telling About Turkeys

My turkey has _eggs_.
Name _Thomas_

Practicing prereading skills is a treat with these terrific turkey booklet pages! In advance, make a copy of page 51 for each child. Then program several index cards with turkey-related words and illustrations (feathers, wattle, caruncle, spurs, beard, eggs, etc.). Place these supplies at a center along with a realistic turkey book, such as *All About Turkeys* by Jim Arnosky. Give each child a page and then ask him to choose one card. Have him write or dictate the word in the space provided on his page. Then ask him to illustrate his sentence. Later, combine the booklet pages into a class book for all to enjoy.

Literacy Center

left-to-right ◄
progression
creative thinking ◄

Turkey Strut

Dramatic-Play
Center

▶ role-playing
▶ creative thinking
▶ gross motor

Encourage youngsters' imaginations with a stroll down to the turkey farm! Stock a center with farmer gear (straw hats, bandanas, vests), turkey gear (feather headbands, cone-shaped party hats for beaks), and plastic buckets that will hold imaginary turkey feed. Explain to youngsters that *poults* (baby turkeys) make a *cheep-cheep* and a *kee-kee-kee* sound. Further explain that a *hen yelps* and a *tom* says *gobble, gobble.* Invite several students to don the farmer gear while several others dress as turkeys. Have the farmers sprinkle some feed around on the ground and call the turkeys to dinner. Then encourage the little turkeys to strut, scratch, and peck at the ground in search of food as they make turkey sounds. If desired, play your favorite turkey–strutting music.

Kee-kee!

Feathery Friend

Art
Center

▶ fine motor
▶ creative expression

"Wattle" you know—these funny bird paintings are sure to teach your youngsters about a turkey's body parts. In advance, collect several feathers, tempera paints, crayons, red tissue paper pieces, and orange yarn pieces. Mask out the sentence starter on a copy of page 51 and then make a class supply of copies. Place the supplies and a picture of a real turkey at a center. Invite each child to color her turkey's head and body. Next, have her glue a yarn *caruncle* on the top of its beak and a tissue paper *wattle* on its neck. Then have her dip a different feather into each paint color to brush on beautiful turkey feathers.

Name McKenna

Use with "Telling About Turkeys" on page 49 and "Feathery Friend" on page 50.

My turkey has _____.

Name _____

Positively Pizza!

There's no doubt about it—pizza is a hot topic! So set up the following centers and serve your little ones plenty of valuable learning skills.

by Sherri Lynn Kuntz

All Covered With Sauce

Literacy Center

▶ exposure to print
▶ letter/number recognition

Tempt your youngsters with some pizza sauce prewriting practice! In advance, program name, alphabet, or phone number cards similar to the ones shown. Laminate the cards for durability; then place them at the center. For each child, use waxed paper to line a shallow pizza pan or baking sheet. Then add a thin layer of pizza sauce. When a child visits this center, have him choose a card and then use his finger to squiggle or form the matching letters or numbers in the sauce. What a tasty way to practice printing!

767-8538   B E N   Sam

Toppings to Go!

Math Center

▶ sorting
▶ matching

This pizza slice sorting activity is topped with lots of fun! In advance, ask your local pizza shop to donate six small take-out boxes. To prepare, make six copies of the pizza slice pattern and two copies of the topping patterns on page 55 and then cut them out. Glue a different topping to each pizza box as shown. Then glue a matching topping in the center of each pizza slice. Place the slices on a paper plate at the center along with the boxes. To play, have youngsters sort the slices into the appropriate boxes. For an added challenge, invite them to sort the slices in a set amount of time. Get ready, get set, sort!

Tip the Scale With Toppings!

Just "weight" and see all the discovery learning that takes place in this center! In advance, place an empty margarine container on each tray of a balance scale. In separate bowls, provide a variety of toppings, such as pepperoni slices, pineapple chunks, and black olives. (Also provide spoons for juicy toppings.) When a child visits this center, have her select a topping and then scoop a spoonful (or small handful) of it into one of the margarine tubs. Then have her choose another topping and add it to the second tub until the scale balances. Invite her to continue exploring with all the toppings in this manner. Hey, this is the heaviest topping in town!

Discovery Center

weight exploration ◄
observation ◄

Hands Up for Pizza Dough

"Knead" a new twist in your sensory area? Then toss in some fun using stretchy, soft pizza dough! In advance, have parent volunteers donate several rolls of refrigerated pizza dough (or prepare your favorite dough recipe). Put the dough, pizza pans, rolling pins, and aprons at your sensory area, along with a bowl of flour. Then invite youngsters to pull, knead, roll, and flatten the dough. Your little pizza bakers are sure to be up to their elbows in enthusiasm!

Sensory Center

texture exploration ◄
fine motor ◄

53

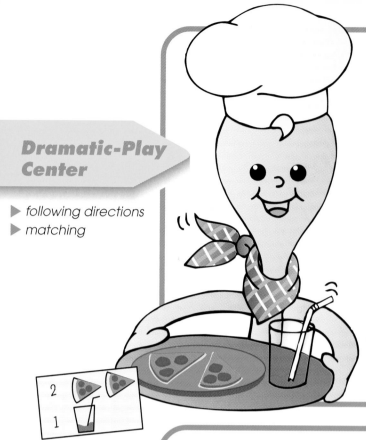

Dramatic-Play Center

▶ *following directions*
▶ *matching*

Pizza Parlor Play

This dramatic-play idea is sure to deliver extra large learning fun! In advance, create pretend drinks by squirting a different color of glue into the bottom of each of several clear plastic cups. Insert a flexible drinking straw; then set the cups aside to dry for several days. Next, cut out several pizza slice shapes and an assortment of toppings from craft foam. Finally, make order cards by programming several index cards similar to the ones shown. Place all of the supplies in the center along with trays and take-out pizza boxes. Invite students to take turns ordering and making pizzas. Here you go, sir. That's a large pizza with extra matching and following directions—but no anchovies!

Art Center

▶ *fine motor*
▶ *creative expression*
▶ *following directions*

Pizzas Fresh From the Oven!

Tell your little ones that they're making this scrumptious pizza pie art and they just might create seconds! When a child visits the center, have her write her name on the back of a paper plate. Then guide each child through the directions below to create her own original pizza slice. When the project is dry, personalize each child's plate and write her pizza description on it. Display the projects on a red-and-white checked background. Mmmm, look at those cheesy pizza slices!

Materials needed for each child:
1 brown construction paper triangle (pizza slice)
one 9" paper plate
red tempera paint (pizza sauce)
paintbrush
yellow-tinted glue (melted cheese)
a variety of art supplies (toppings)
real oregano

Directions:
1. Glue the pizza slice to the center of the paper plate.
2. Paint some sauce onto the pizza slice.
3. Squeeze melted cheese onto the pizza slice.
4. Add toppings.
5. Sprinkle oregano on the pizza slice.

Sherri's pizza

I like green peppers and meatballs on my pizza. And lots of cheese!

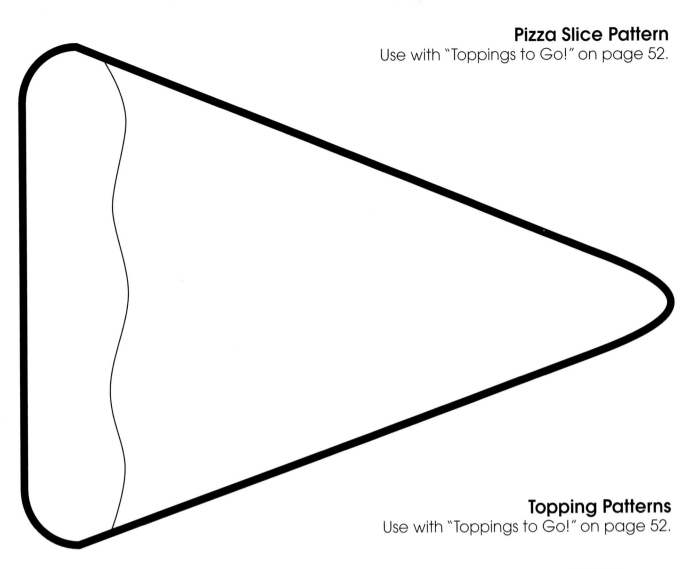

Topping Patterns
Use with "Toppings to Go!" on page 52.

pepperoni

green peppers

cheese

black olives

ham

mushrooms

It's a PB&J Day!

Spread on a thick layer of exploration fun with these not-too-sticky PB&J center ideas.

by Cindy K. Daoust

For safety, please check for peanut allergies before using the activities in this unit.

Literacy Center

▶ *experience with text*
▶ *sorting*

Label It Fun!

Your little PB&J lovers are sure to get lots of prereading practice with this label-sorting activity. In advance, request food labels or pictures of foods that contain peanut butter, jelly, or bread. To prepare, trim the labels and then cut out three large shapes from bulletin board paper to resemble a brown peanut, a white bread slice, and a scoop of purple jelly. Place the paper cutouts and the labels at the center. Then invite a small group of children to sort the labels by placing each one on the appropriate cutout.

Peanut Butter

Peanut Butter Cookies

Peanut Butter Crackers

Math Center

▶ *matching*
▶ *counting*

Name Jack

PB&J Race Finish

PEANUT BUTTER

Peanut Start

Jelly Start

Peanut

Jelly

PB&J Race!

Shift youngsters' shape discrimination skills into high gear with this racing game! Color and cut out two copies of the card patterns on page 59 and place them in a paper lunch bag. Then make a class supply of the gameboard patterns on page 59 and display the gameboards, cards, lunch bag, and several peanuts and purple pom-poms at a center. To begin the race, a child places a peanut and a pom-pom game piece on the starting line. Next, he selects a card from the bag and moves the matching game piece forward one space. He continues in this manner until one game piece reaches the finish line. Finally, he records the race results by coloring each peanut and jelly space crossed. Challenge the child to play a second game on the other half of the gameboard and then compare the results of the two races!

Squishy Slates

Scoop up some gooey tactile fun with these no-mess PB&J scribbling slates. To create an individual slate, fill a snack-sized resealable plastic bag with one tablespoon each of peanut butter and jelly. Press the air out of the bag as you seal it, and then use masking tape to secure the seal. Invite little ones to swirl the PB&J and use their fingers to draw or write on their slates. No mess here—just clean, squishy fun!

Plant a Peanut

Watch students' observation skills grow with this peanut-planting experience. Display soil, pebbles, raw unsalted peanuts, and a class supply of clear nine-ounce plastic cups at a center. Direct each child to place a handful of pebbles in the bottom of one cup and then half-fill the cup with soil and press several peanuts into the soil. Next, have her add a small amount of water to the cup and place it near a sunny window. Each day, encourage her to visit the center, water her plant, and observe any changes. (*After five days, roots should appear at the bottom of the cup. After eight days, a sprout should be pushing up through the soil. Then, a stalk, leaves, and yellow flowers should grow. Finally, after about 50 days, the stalk will begin to push down into the soil and develop into a peanut pod. One plant can grow several peanut pods.*)

Peanut Pod Toss

Strengthen hand-eye coordination with this peanut-and-jelly-tossin' game. To prepare, decorate a large paper bag to resemble a peanut character as shown. Next, use tape to create a line on the floor. Then place the bag at a predetermined distance from the line. Place a heavy object inside the bag to prevent it from tipping. Then gather ten purple pom-poms and ten unshelled peanuts. Have each child stand behind the line and try to toss a peanut or a pom-pom into the top of the bag. Continue until each child has had a turn. When finished, have youngsters empty the bag to count the peanuts and pom-poms. For a variation, encourage older children to toss the peanuts and pom-poms into the peanut character's cutout mouth. Ready? Set. Toss!

PB&J Hurray!

Shake up a familiar song as your youngsters spread the rhythmic sounds of this catchy tune. In advance, create a few shakers by placing several real peanuts inside empty plastic peanut butter containers. Then invite youngsters to use the shakers to count the beats as they sing the song below.

(sung to the tune of "Three Blind Mice")

PB&J, PB&J!
Peanut butter and jelly!
Peanut butter and jelly!
Scoop and spread them on bread so neat.
Chomp a big bite. It can't be beat.
Have you ever had such a tasty treat?
It's PB&J!

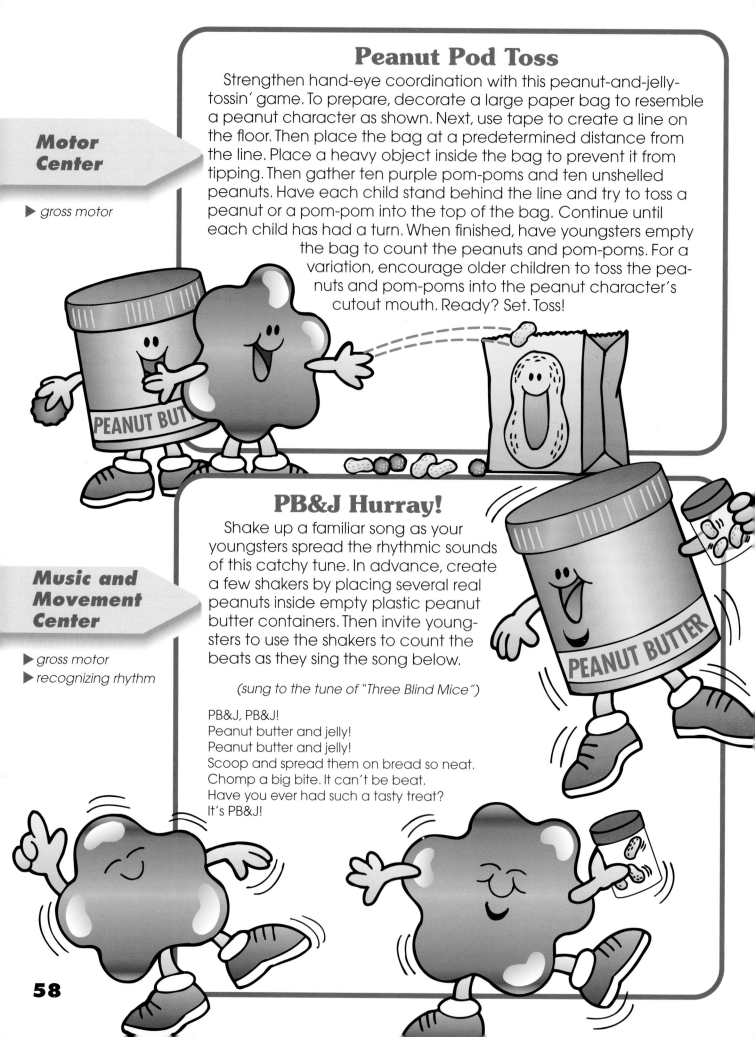

58

Name _____

PB&J Race
Finish

PEANUT BUTTER

Peanut
Start

Jelly
Start

Name _____

PB&J Race
Finish

PEANUT BUTTER

Peanut
Start

Jelly
Start

©2001 The Education Center, Inc. • *Centered on Learning* • *Fall* • TEC3517

Peanut

Peanut

Peanut

Peanut

Jelly

Jelly

Jelly

Jelly

59

Teddy Bear Time

Your little ones will "bear-ly" notice they're reinforcing skills across the curriculum when they visit these terrific teddy bear centers.

by Mackie Rhodes

Literacy Center

▶ matching uppercase and lowercase letters

Think, Think, Think

Teddy Bear always knows the answer to this letter-recognition partner game. To prepare, place a teddy bear and a set of uppercase and lowercase plastic letters at the center. Invite a pair of children to spread the letters on the floor. Have one child close her eyes while her partner hides a letter underneath the teddy bear. Then direct the first child to pick up the bear, find the hidden letter, and search for its matching uppercase or lowercase letter. The game continues in this manner until all the letters have been matched. For younger children, use two sets of uppercase letters.

Math Center

▶ counting
▶ one-to-one correspondence
▶ fine motor

Paws for Teddy

Count on this center to reinforce counting skills and "paws-itively" delight your little ones! Make several brown construction paper copies of the bear card pattern on page 63. Laminate the cards and display them at a center with dice, play dough, and a supply of dried beans. Have each child flatten two small balls of dough and place one on each paw on her bear card. Next, instruct her to roll one die and push the corresponding number of beans into one paw to resemble the bear's claws. Then have her roll the die again to determine a number of claws to push into the second paw. Encourage her to remove the claws and play again for more "paws-on" counting practice!

Textured Teddy Tootsies

This matching activity gets your youngsters in touch with textures! Make two to four construction paper copies of the bear card pattern on page 63 and then laminate the cards for durability. Attach a small piece of self-adhesive Velcro® (hook side) onto each paw. Next, prepare sets of textured paws by cutting pairs of circles from various textures, such as sandpaper, faux fur, felt, and corduroy. Then attach pieces of Velcro (loop side) to the backs of each pair. Hide one paw of each pair in the bag. To play, one child attaches a textured paw to a bear card. Another child feels inside the bag to find the matching paw and then attaches it to the bear's paw. Play continues until all the paws have been matched. Go ahead and touch those tootsies!

Science Center

tactile discrimination ◄
matching ◄

Please Feed the Bears

Invite your little ones to feast on visual discrimination skills at the bears' brunch! Simply add colored rice to your sensory table along with bear-shaped counters, pom-poms, sifters, and scoops. Invite little ones to stir, scoop, and sift. As children find the bears and pom-poms, encourage them to sort and count them into corresponding labeled bowls.

Sensory Center

visual discrimination ◄
color recognition ◄
sorting ◄

Bubbly Bears

These tactile teddy bears will quickly become the center of attention! Make a class supply of the teddy bear pattern on page 64. Next, tape 9" x 12" pieces of bubble wrap on a tabletop. Have each child paint a piece of bubble wrap with brown paint and then press his bear facedown onto the painted surface. Direct the child to gently lift his paper and then set it aside to dry. Finally, invite him to cut out his bear and use various craft materials to add desired details. Display these "grrrrreat" teddy bears for all to enjoy!

Art Center

▶ tactile exploration
▶ following directions
▶ creativity

Teddy Bears on the Move

Teddy bears large and small enjoy moving to this familiar rhyme! In advance, color, cut apart, and laminate a copy of the word cards on page 63. Attach a small piece of Sticky-Tac® to the back of each card. Next, print the first verse of the teddy bear rhyme on a chart as shown. Then invite a student volunteer to choose a word card to place in the blank space on the chart. Have the students at the center recite and act out the rhyme. Repeat the activity with each of the remaining word cards. Teddy Bear, Teddy Bear, read and do!

Music and Movement Center

▶ gross motor
▶ listening
▶ following directions

Teddy Bear, Teddy Bear,

 Dance _____ around.

Teddy Bear, Teddy Bear,

Touch the ground.

Teddy Bear, Teddy Bear,

Show your shoe.

Teddy Bear, Teddy Bear,

That will do!

Bear Card Pattern

Use with "Paws for Teddy" on page 60 and "Textured Teddy Tootsies" on page 61.

©2001 The Education Center, Inc. • *Centered on Learning* • *Fall* • TEC3517

Word Cards

Use with "Teddy Bears on the Move" on page 62.

Turn	Stomp
Jump	Dance
Tiptoe	Run
Hop	March

Teddy Bear Pattern
Use with "Bubbly Bears" on page 62.